SELF KNOWLEDGE & SELF REALIZATION

Sri Nisargadatta Maharaj

Edited by Jean Dunn

ISBN 978-93-48143-04-4

Table of Contents

FOREWORD

My preceptor Shree Sadguru Nisargadatta Maharaj, the Author of the present collection of homilies is a member of the spiritual lineage of the Navanathas. Shree Revananath, the last of the Navanathas' founded his own sect in the south with Kadsiddheshwar as his chosen disciples. The latter initiated Shree Gurulingajangama Maharaja along with other disciples into the spiritual secrets of his sect. Shree Bhausaheb Umadikar and Shree Rambhau Yeragattikar were the renouned disciples of Shree Gurulingajangam Maharaj. Inchegeri Sampradaya to which Nisargadatta Maharaj belongs was founded by Shree Sadguru Bhausaheb Maharaj the elder of the two disciples of Gurulingajangam Maharaja.

Introduction of Bhajan four times a day is mainly responsible for the healthy growth of this Sampradaya and it was done by the founder himself and it is scrupulously followed by all the devout followers of the Sampradaya. Prominent among the disciples of Shree Bhausaheb Maharaj were the late Dr. R. D. Ranade, Shree Amburao Maharaj, Shree Siddharameshwar Maharaja and Shree Siddhalingayya Swamy, Shree Girimalleshwar Maharaja of these, Shree Siddharameshwar Maharaj chose a few prominent places such as Bombay, Sholapur, Kolhapur etc. for the spread of 'Bhakti' and 'spiritual Knowledge' and was active from 1924 to the last moment of his life.

Shree Nisargadatta Maharaja is a disciple of Shree Siddharameshwar Maharaja. He was born on the auspicious day of Hanumana Jayanti in 1897 and was hence named Maruti. Since his childhood he was deeply interest- ed in religious activities and philosophical literature. Visiting the temples of Gods and the observance of religious fasts and traditional rituals increased his thirst for the Vision of God. He was then a noted businessman in Bombay, but was not at all interested in the business. In a few years time he bade good bye to the business to utilise his time in the quest of the Ultimate. He approached the great saint Shree Siddharameshwar Maharaja and was intiated by him. On the advise of his preceptor he gave up his earlier practices of fasting and rituals. Within less than a years' time he was ripe for holding meetings for religious discourses. It was at Malavan, his native place that he made the beginning of his Life Mission.

After the demise of his preceptor, the intensity of the urge for self-realisation reached its limit and he left for Pandharpur without giving thought even for a moment to what would happen to those that were dependent on him; and spent about six months in visiting various holy places i= the North and South.

Shree Nisargadatta Maharaj has no patience with miracles. He is convinced that they are a positive hindrance to spiritual progress. He says "The aspirant should take his Pure Self as his preceptor and persue with sincerity and intense love". He further says "Your preceptor tells you that 'You are Pure Consciousness, and Pure Divinity'; believe in his word and proceed with your Sadhāna. You must see the Light. Be kind to all living beings. Do not hate nor envy anybody. Be straight and courteous in your behaviour. There is only one God and that is 'Self-Knowledge'. Two collections of his teachings super-saturated with spiritual knowledge are published in Marathi; the first one is 'Atmagnyāna Ani Paramatmayoga' and is the basis of the present

English adaptation; the second " Ishwar Gnyāna Swarūpa Ani Sāt-Swarāpagñyana" was published in 1960.

People from different walks of life come to him for guidance. He does not recognise any distinctions of Caste and Religion. Portraits of great Saints of different religions find an honoured place in his sanctuary and are worshiped every day along with that of his own preceptor. He never accepts any gift from any one; nor does he allow any one to serve him. He says "I do not want any thing from you, on the contrary you can ask for any thing from me. You should give me all your vices and weaknesses, you should not take them back from here".

As stated above this book-let contains English adaptations of the book "Atmagnyāna and Paramatmayoga" which is widely read by all Marathi knowing people. In my discussions with a number of my friends and acquaintances who do not know Marathi I found that I myself could not explain these teachings either in Hindi or English. This, inability of mine prompted me to think of an English adaptations of the discourses. My friend

Shree P. T. Phadole, Registrar Elphinstone College, Bombay, came to my help and introduced me to Prof. V. M. Kulkarni, who is a disciple of Gurudeva Dr. R. D. Ranade, Prof. Kulkarni on knowing my intention voluntarily undertook the work himself and has done it so well. I am very much greatful to him for the same.

The brochure is meant mainly for those who aspire to know something of the spiritual life. Howsoever extensive and detailed a book may be it can never be a substitute for a direct discussion with the enlightened person. I, therefore, pray that those who have any difficulties should get them clarified in person from my preceptor. He is easy to approach and will be delighted to discuss spiritual matters with every one who desires to do so. He has reached the final goal of spiritual life and is forever free from the cycle of birth and death, and hence ageless; yet empirically he enters his 67 th year on the 8th of April 1963. On this occassion I pray Him that we, his disciples be given the opportunity to serve him for many years to come.

Om-Tat-Sat.

Shree Nisargadatta Ashram
Vanamali Bhuwan
10th Khatwadi Bombay-4.
8th April 1963

Ram Narayan Chavan.

APOLOGIA

The following lines are like bracket signs on the keyboard of a type-writer. They mean nothing. One may tap them only if they serve the purpose. My only excuse for scribbling them here is that Shri Nisargadatta Maharaj bids me do so and I obey.

From the account of his spiritual progress recorded in the text, it is obvious that he is a mystic to be mentioned with respect. He has an easy access to all the four great yogas though he lays particular stress on the easiest of them viz. The Nāmajapa Yoga—as is clear from the last two paragraphs in the discourse on Gayatri Chhanda. The final goal is the realization of the Identity of the individual soul with the Supreme Being. His sole interest as a saint lies in guiding men on the Path way to God. Undoubtedly, ignorance is the greatest hurdle that blocks the path of the common man to spiritual life, yet one cannot ignore the part played by physical sufferings in this respect. More often than not these sufferings are responsible for his indifference. Alleviation of pain and misery is as important as is the removal of ignorance.

There is nothing intrinsically wrong with the Siddhis; and no Rajayogi has ever said that their use in the service of humanity would be an obstacle in the way of Self-Realisation. It would be, this humble scribe feels, an ideal combination of Raj Yoga and Karmāyoga. One would sincerely wish, Shri Nisargadatta Maharaja chose a few of his trusted disciples for this mission as the great saint Ramakrishna Paramhansa had done in the case of Swami Vivekananda. May be, it is already in his own mission, as an item; and if so, it should receive the attention it deserves.

It is very rarely that such a queer, though humble, suggestion is put forth before a mystic. But it is a matter of bracket signs after all. They need not be made use of it out of time.

V. M. Kulearni.

ABRIDGED PREFACE

(*of the Original Marathi book*)

I first came in contact with Shri Sadguru Nisargadatta Maharaja (his original name being Shri Marutirao Shivarama Kambli) at the fag end of the year 1933. We, all of us co-disciples, were singing our night prayers with our preceptor (Shri Siddharameshwar Maharaja), in the hall of one of our senior co-disciples Shri Krishnarao R. Pathare (Solicitor) at Gamdevi; and we used to meet later on as co-disciples. But I came in intimate contact with him only at the begining of 1941. I take it to be a great favour of Shri Sadguru Siddharameshwar Maharaja that I was blesssd by the company of an enlightened soul to guide me at the highest level in my spiritual pursuit after his departure (only physical, of course). In recognition of this favour whatever I say is a heart felt expression inspired by the Guru himself; and it is his nector sweet voice, not mine. I venture to write this preface only to honour the loving insistance of the disciples of Shri Nisargadatta Maharaja. A preface to a book like the present one is not the proper place to dwell on the personal relations at length. Hence, it is better to resist the temptation to go ahead with it.

This book begins with the discourse on the Great Principle. "There should one enter into discussion", says Ramdas "Where a satisfactory end can be visualised; and this can best be interpreted as that alone should be discussed which is the root cause of all discussions and where all discussions come to an end. “The apperception of the “I” in one’s own being is the consummation of all knowledge, while the perception of the “Ego” there is the greatest calamity” (Yoga Väsishtha). The realisation of not “I” but ‘Thou’ O, God is the veritable salvation; The assertion of the ‘ego’ is the root cause of all suffering. This basic fact has been exquisitely explained in a number of discourses in the present book. Though no references have been quoted in support of the arguments and statements in point, a sympathetic and wise reader will certainly be reminded of different works and sayings of great saints while reading.

Though the language of some of the discourses such as ‘The Lilä of God’ ‘the Unitive Life’, Gayatri hymn’ and etc. is not within the easy grasp of the common man, the rhythem in itself is enough to hold him spell bound; (and in course of time he is sure to grasp the sense as well) for ‘The language may change, but the meaning is not lost; what matters above all is the meaning itself’ (Dasabodha).

The conviction that “I am not the body and hence am not like it; I am the soul, am the Brahman” is the very basis of spiritual life. In social interaction when angry, a one warns the other ‘Not a word about me, mind you; I am not what I look’. Similarly as the saying goes there is no remedy to change one’s nature. This and other similar proverbs have come from the mouth of the learned people. Here ‘nature’ stands for the core of the conscious principle, the eternal supreme soul and its sacred power. If the supreme soul be eternal, how can its power be evanescent? This energy plays the game of cosmic display for a while and disappears only to emerge again. This its rhythemic process goes on forever. That energy that duration (in the Bergsonian sense) is also called the feet of the saints. This duration is immeasurable. For the sun rise, the very measurement thereof, is not there at all. Still this experience (Anu Bhava i.e. The atom has 'become' This world) is not always to be had in its pure form and is, hence, to be called Māyā. As in the waking state so too in deep sleep the soul experiences a world sin-generis; and what are its constituents? The Universal soul, the atom of atoms becomes active and shines forth as surrounded by the universe. Its first ray of light is the ether and the rest is pumped hard into it. The saint is always aware of this fact and hence is cautious in his behaviour. "In the dreams, we feel we are awake. The same is true of the intimations of the spiritual experiences in the beginning; but that too is dream again; it is an hallucination" (Dasabodha). Hence, in any eventuality, the saints are always calm and composed and outspoken. But to attain to this status one must grow self-less and indifferent. One must renounce the evanescent for the eternal. The sense of renunciation comes not of the saffron coloured garb but of indifference to the body; The conviction that I am not the body but the great soul is the real sign of spiritual knowledge". (Shankarāchārya - Sadachār). "The saints have no expectations nor pride nor interest nor again duality; All are equal for them; They are composed and their mind is ever attuned to Mine" (E, B.) This point is exquisitely expounded in the discourses on the 'Divine Vision and the Devotee; 'Devotion to Balkrishna and his care', 'Spiritual knowledge and the Pacification of the desire to know' and etc.

Is there anything in the universe that does not owe its being to Pranava? All that is and appears is an expression of the Pranava. He alone permeates through and through everything in the universe. Is it not indeed surprising that the loving and lovable Pranava should in loving anger expect to get satisfaction in salutation? This is lucidly brought out in 'The Gayatri Hymns', 'Know what? and 'the Spiritual Bliss'.

To wit, every discourse goes to the very root of the subject and is strewn with intense devotion, enlightenment and spiritual resignation. This has made the book facinating, and unique. The reader is sure to meet with enlightenment and joy while going through the book. The discourse on "Spiritual knowledge and the pacification of the desire to know' may be read first with profit. If a careful and repeated study of the 'Floral offerings' be undertaken along with careful study of the whole book, the aspirant, I am sure, will reap the high harvest of spiritual knowledge with the grace of Shri Sadguru Siddharameshwar Maharaja.

5, Tara Temple Lane, Lamington Road,
Bombay No. 7, Ghaitea Suddha Pratipada,
Saka 1880. Date: 21-3-58.

EDITOR'S NOTES

The original script for these writings of Sri Nisargadatta Maharaj was written in the Marathi language and called "Atmagnyana and Paramatmayoga".

A translation in English by Vasudeo Madhav Kulkarni, at the time a Professor at Elphinstone College, Bombay, India, was published on April 8, 1963, under Maharaj's title, translated as "Self Knowledge and Self Realization".

Professor Kulkarni's adaptation was published with a foreword by Shree Ram Narayan Chavhan, at Shree Nisargadatta Ashram, Vanmali Bhavan, 10th Khetwadi, Bombay 4, India.

Professor Kulkarni's translation was printed in India by J.D. Desai, Pashtra Vaibhav Press, 273 Vithalbhai Patel Rd., Girgaon, Bombay 4, India.

FOREWORD BY JEAN DUNN

I first purchased this little book in Bombay in 1978, and while it was difficult to read, it was so very dear that I decided to edit it, making it easier to understand. I did this for myself, and just recently, after lending it to others, and on their insistence, I decided to print a few copies for those on the spiritual path. I tried and failed to trace the original publishers.

While Sri Nisargadatta Maharaj, in his last few years, would not entertain any questions about experiences in this "dream world", I feel that this book tells of his own spiritual path and experiences.

Nisargadatta Maharaj was from the spiritual lineage of the Navanathas.

He was born in Bombay in 1897, and was brought up on a farm in Kandalgaon, a village south of Bombay. He had an alert, inquisitive mind, and was deeply interested in religious and philosophical matters. After the death of his father, he moved to Bombay in 1918, and in 1924 married Sumatibai, who bore him a son and three daughters.

Although he started life in Bombay as an office clerk, he soon went out on his own and started a small business, and in a few years he owned several small shops. A hunger for truth grew in him, and in 1933, due to a friend's urging, he approached the great Saint, Sri Siddharameshwar

Maharaj, and was initiated by him.

After the death of his Guru in 1936, the urge for Self-realization reached its zenith, and in 1937 he abandoned his family and businesses and took to the life of a wandering monk. On his way to the Himalayas, where he intended to spend the rest of his life, he met a brother disciple who convinced him that a life of dispassion in action would be more spiritually fruitful.

Returning to Bombay, he found only one store remaining of his business ventures. For the sake of his family he conducted the business but devoted all his energy to spiritual sadhana. He built himself a mezzanine floor as a place for meditation (this is the room where we all used to gather to listen to him talk).

In his own words, "When I met my Guru, he told me, 'You are not what you take yourself to be. Find out what you are. Watch the sense I AM, find your real Self...' I did as he told me. All my spare time I would spend looking at myself in silence...and what a difference it made, and how soon! It took me only three years to realize my true nature." His message to us was simple and direct with no propounding of scriptures or doctrines. "You are the Self here and now! Stop imagining yourself to be something else. Let go your attachment to the unreal."

Maurice Frydman, a Polish devotee, often acted as translator and the questions and answers were so interesting that tape recordings were made, and in 1973 these were published under the title "I Am That". . As a result, readers from many different countries came to Bombay seeking the spiritual guidance of Sri Maharaj.

From 1978 to 1981, when Sri Maharaj died from cancer of the throat, his talks were so much deeper than in the previous years that, with the help of a few other devotees, the tape recordings were again resumed and I transcribed and edited them, with the blessings of Sri Maharaj, and these were published under the titles of "Seeds of Consciousness" and "Prior to Consciousness"; both titles were suggested by Sri Maharaj.

JEAN DUNN

DIVINE VISION AND THE DEVOTEE

Divine vision means acquaintance with, and crystalline understanding of, the universal energy. God and the devotee are one, in his very nature the devotee is identical with God. So long as one has not realized God, one does not know what justice and injustice are, but with realization the devotee comes to know the distinction between justice and injustice, the essential and the contingent, the eternal and the evanescent, and this leads to his emancipation.

The divine vision eliminates individuality; the manifest is clearly distinguished from the unmanifest. When the sense of individuality is replaced by that of impersonal consciousness the devotee knows that he is pure consciousness. Manifestation is pure consciousness manifesting itself in all the different names and forms; the spiritually enlightened take part in it sportively, knowing that it is only the play of universal consciousness.

The name and form of the spiritually enlightened Saint experiences the pangs and sorrows of life, but not their sting. He is neither moved nor perturbed by the pleasures and pains, nor the profits and losses of the world. He is thus in a position to direct others. His behavior is guided exclusively by the sense of justice.

The temporal life must continue, with all its complex interactions, but the Saint is ever aware that it is only the pure consciousness that is expressing itself in different names and forms, and it continues to do so, in ever new forms. To him, the unbearable events of the world are just a tame and harmless affair; he remains unmoved in world-shaking events.

At first people, through pride, simply ignore him, but their subsequent experiences draw them toward him. God, as justice incarnate, has neither relations nor belongings of His own; peace and happiness are, as it were, His only treasure. The formless, divine consciousness cannot have any thing as its own interest.

This is the temporal outline of the Bhakta.

THE SOUL, THE WORLD, BRAHMAN AND SELF REALIZATION

The consciousness of one's own being, of the world, and of its supporting primal force are experienced all at once. Awareness of one's own being does not mean here the physical consciousness of oneself as an individual, but implies the mystery of existence. Prior to this, in the ignorance of one's own being, there is no experience of Brahman as being there. But the moment one is aware of being, he is directly aware of the world and Brahman, too.

At the stage prior to this cosmic awareness, the self and its experiences are limited to the worldly life. This worldly life starts with birth and ends in death. To become aware of ourself, the world and God all of a sudden is a great mystery indeed. It is an unexpected gain; it is an absorbing and a mysterious event, extremely significant and great, but it brings with it the responsibility of Self-preservation, sustenance and Self development as well, and no one can avoid it.

One who leads his life without ever wondering about who or what he is accepts the traditional genealogical history as his own and follows the customary religious and other activities according to tradition. He leads his life with the firm conviction that the world was there prior to his existence, and that it is real; because of this conviction he behaves as he does, gathering possessions and treasures for himself, even knowing that at the time of death he will never see them again. Knowing that none of this will even be remembered after death, still his greed and avarice operate unabated until death.

When we concentrate our attention on the origin of thought, the thought process itself comes to an end; there is a hiatus, which is pleasant, and again the process starts. Turning from the external world and enjoying the objectless bliss, the mind feels that the world of objects is not for it. Prior to this experience the unsatiating sense enjoyments constantly challenged the mind to satisfy them, but from the inward turn onwards its interest in them begins to fade.

Once the internal bliss is enjoyed, the external happiness loses its charm. One who has tasted the inward bliss is naturally loving and free from envy, contented and happy with others' prosperity, friendly and innocent and free from deceit. He is full of the mystery and wonder of the bliss. One who has realized the Self can never inflict pain on other.

LIFE DIVINE AND THE SUPREME SELF

With heartfelt love and devotion, the devotee propitiates God; and when he is blessed with His vision and grace, he feels ever happy in His presence. The constant presence establishes a virtual identity between the two. While seeking the presence of the Supreme Soul, the Bhakta renounces all associations in his life, from the meanest to the best, and having purged his being of all associations, he automatically wins the association with the Supreme Self. One who has attained to the position of unstinted emancipation can never be disliked by others, for the people themselves are the very Self-luminous soul, though ignorant of the fact.

In this world of immense variety, different beings are suffering from different kinds of ailments, and yet they are not prepared to give up the physical frame, even when wailing under physical and mental pain. If this be so, then men will not be so short-sighted as to avoid their savior, the enlightened soul.

That overflowing reservoir of bliss, the beatific soul, does confer only bliss on the people by his loving light. Even the atmosphere around him heartens the suffering souls. He is like the waters of a lake that gives nourishment to the plants and trees around the brink and the grass and fields nearby. The Saint gives joy and sustaining energy to the people around him.

THE ASPIRANT AND SPIRITUAL THOUGHT

Spiritual thought is of the Highest. This seeking of the Highest is called the "first half" by the Saints. A proper understanding of this results in the vision of God, and eventually matures into the certainty of the true nature of the Self in the "latter half".

One who takes to the path of the spirit starts with contemplation and propitiation. It is here, for the first time, that he finds some joy in prayer and worship. At this preliminary stage he gets the company of co-aspirants. Reading of the lives and works of past incarnations of God, of Rishis, of Saints and Sages, singing the glories of the Name, visiting temples, and a constant meditation on these result in the photic and phonic experiences of the mystic life; his desires are satisfied to an extent now. Thinking that he has had the vision of God, he intensifies his efforts of fondly remembering the name of God and His worship. In this state of the mind, the Bhakta quite frequently has a glimpse of his cherished deity, which he takes to be the divine vision and is satisfied with it. At this juncture, he is sure to come into contact with a Saint.

The Saint, and now his preceptor, makes it plain to him that what he has had is not the real vision, which is beyond the said experiences, and is only to be had through Self-Realization. At this point, the aspirant reaches the stage of the meditator. In the beginning, the

Sadhaka is instructed into the secrets of his own person, and of the indwelling spirit; the meaning and nature of prana, the various plexuses, and the nature and arousal of the Kundalini, and the nature of the Self. Later on, he comes to know of the origin of the five elements, their activity, radiation, and merits and defects. Meanwhile his mind undergoes the process of purification and acquires composure, and this the Sadhaka experiences through the deep-laid subtle center of the Indweller; he also knows how and why it is there, only that the deiform element is kindled. This knowledge transforms him into the pure, eternal, and spiritual form of a SadGuru who is now in a position to initiate others into the secrets of the spirit. The stage of Sadhakahood ends here.

As the great Saint Tukarama said, the aspirant must put in ceaseless efforts in the pursuit of spiritual life. Thoughts must be utilized for Self-Knowledge. He must be alert and watchful in ascertaining the nature of this "I" that is involved in the affairs of pleasure and pain arising out of sense experience.

We must know the nature of the active principle lest its activities be led astray. We should not waste our energies in useless pursuits, but should use those energies in the pursuit of the Self and achieve identity with God. Spiritual life is so great, so deep, so immense, that energy pales into insignificance before it, yet this energy tries to understand it again and again. Those who try to understand it with the help of the intellect are lost to it. Rare is the one who, having concentrated on the source atom of the cosmic energy, enjoys the bliss of spiritual contemplation. But there are scores of those who take themselves to be spiritually inspired and perfect beings. They expect the common herd to honor and respect their every word. The ignorant people rush towards them for spiritual succor and do their bidding. In fact, the pseudo-Saints are caught in a snare of greed, hence what the people get in return is not the blessings of satisfaction, but ashes.

The self-styled man of God, speaking ad nauseum about spiritual matters, thinks himself to be perfect, but others are not so sure. As regards a Saint, on the other hand, men are on the lookout for ways to serve him more and more, but as the ever-contented soul, steeped in beatitude, desires nothing, they are left to serve in their own way, which they do with enthusiasm, and they never feel the pressure.

Greatness is always humble, loving, silent and satisfied. Happiness, tolerance, forbearance, composure and other allied qualities must be known by everyone; just as one experiences bodily states such as hunger, thirst, etc., one. must, with equal ease, experience in oneself the characteristics connoted by the word "Saint". As we know for certain that we need no more sleep, no more food, at a given moment, so too we can be sure of the above characteristics from direct experience. One can then recognize their presence in others with the same ease. This is the test and experience of a tried spiritual leader.

THE MYSTIC

The blissful mystic clearly sees the difference between his characteristics before and after realization. All that is transient has an origin in time and is subject to change and destruction, while he is free from change and can never perish. The unchanging one views the ever-changing world as a game.

All the characteristics of the Saint naturally spring from his experience. As there are no desires left in him, nothing in the world of sense can ever tempt him, he lives in the fearless majesty of Self-realization. He is moved to pity by the unsuccessful struggle of those tied down to bodily identity and their striving for the satisfaction of their petty interests. Even the great events of the world are just surface lines to him; the number of these lines that appear and disappear is infinite.

Individuals are only the faint streaks of these lines, and only as such lines are they recognized. When the streaks vanish there remains nothing to recognize as individuals. The interval between the moment of emergence and the disappearance of a line is what is called life. The wiped-out line can never be seen again.

The Saint who has direct experience of all this is always happy and free from desire. He is convinced that the greatest of the sense experiences is only a momentary affair, impermanence is the very essence of these experiences; hence pain and sorrow, greed and temptation, fear and anxiety can never touch him.

THE LILA OF GOD

Sport or play is natural to God, our experiences are known as the Lila (play) of God. Without any prior intimation, we suddenly have a taste of our own being; excepting this one instance of the taste, we have no knowledge of the nature of the Self. But then, even this bit of experience is hidden away from us. We are forced into a series of activities and experiences: that I am a homosapien, I am a body, my name is such and such, this is my religion, my duty, etc. One action follows another, and there is no rest from them, no escape, we have to see them through. This goes on inevitably, until perchance, it loses all its charm, and we seek the spiritual treasure.

If the purpose of all this be inquired into, we get different accounts from different people. Some claim it is because of the actions of millions of previous lives - but nobody has the direct experience of these past lives; it is obvious that this is fiction.

Dazzled by the ingenious inventions and discoveries of the scientists, some base their interpretation on empirical facts and offer them as explanations, but the suddenly experienced taste of our own being cannot be interpreted in this way. When the world is called by the word Maya or illusion, it is condemned to be mean; when the same thing is called by the words "play of God", it becomes great! In reality the facts are what they are. Who is the recipient of the high designation - who confirms the uselessness for the condemnation - who is He - what name should we give Him after first-hand experience?

That we have experiences is a fact; others tell us about their experiences, we receive information concerning relations, and instruction in the performance of activities, and we organize our behavior accordingly. Someone from these guides initiates us into what is said to be the core of the indwelling Spirit, but that too turns out to be a transient affair. For the acquaintance secured thus does not possess the experiential core of the taste, and the initiator himself proves to be part and parcel of that bit; thus both he and his knowledge are lost to us. Now we are free to go our own way, but for want of the necessary taste, this self-help is equally helpless. We are where we were.

What is it that we call the Lila of God? How are we related to this sporting God whom we saw, talked to, had friendship with, and intense love for. In spite of all this closeness and fondness, what is our relation to Him? All the previous experiences with their peculiarities have vanished. The Lila of God disappears along with the pseudo experience with the advent of the present experience.

THE SPIRITUAL ASPIRANT, THE FIRST MOMENT OF BLISS AND ITS CONTINUOUS GROWTH

The ever-awaited first moment was the moment when I was convinced that I was not an individual at all. The idea of my individuality had set me burning so far. The scalding pain was beyond my capacity to endure; but there is not even a trace of it now, I am no more an individual. There is nothing to limit my being now. The ever-present anxiety and the gloom have vanished and now I am all beatitude, pure knowledge, pure consciousness.

The tumors of innumerable desires and passion were simply unbearable, but fortunately for me, I got hold of the hymn "Hail, Preceptor", and on its constant recitation, all the tumors of passions withered away as with a magic spell!

I am ever free now. I am all bliss, sans spite, sans fear. This beatific conscious form of mine now knows no bounds. I belong to all and everyone is mine. The "all" are but my own individuations, and these together go to make up my beatific being. There is nothing like good or bad, profit or loss, high or low, mine or not mine for me. Nobody opposes me and I oppose none for there is none other than myself. Bliss reclines on the bed of bliss. The repose itself has turned into bliss.

There is nothing that I ought or ought not to do, but my

activity goes on everywhere, every minute. Love and anger are divided equally among all, as are work and recreation. My characteristics of immensity and majesty, my pure energy, and my all, having attained to the golden core, repose in bliss as the atom of atoms. My pure consciousness shines forth in majestic splendor.

Why and how the consciousness became self-conscious is obvious now. The experience of the world is no more of the world as such, but is the blossoming forth of the selfsame conscious principle, God, and what is it? It is pure, primal knowledge, conscious form, the primordial "I" consciousness that is capable of assuming any form it desires. It is designated as God. The world as the divine expression is not for any profit or loss; it is the pure, simple, natural flow of beatific consciousness. There are no distinctions of God and devotee, nor Brahman and Maya. He that meditated on the bliss and peace is himself the ocean of peace and bliss. Glory to the eternal truth, Sat-Guru, the Supreme Self.

DEVOTEE AND THE BLESSINGS OF GOD

The Bhakta pours out his devotion, molds his behavior in every respect in accordance with the will of God. In turn, he finds that God is pleased with him, and this, his conviction, takes him nearer to God and his love and friendship with Him grow richer and richer. The process of surrendering to the will of God in every respect results in His blessings.

One who is blessed by God is a blissful soul. Being at peace with himself, he looks at the objects of enjoyment with perfect indifference. He is content with whatever he has and is glad to see others happy. If a person believes that he is blessed by God and is still unhappy, it is better if he give up this delusion and strive for the coveted Grace with sincerity and honesty.

Divine plenitude and favor is not judged by the objects of sense, but by the internal contentment. This verily is the blessing of God.

THE UNITIVE LIFE

Him have I seen now whom I so earnestly desired to see, I met myself. The meeting requires an extremely difficult and elaborate preparation.

I pined to see the most beloved one. It was impossible to do without it, I was sure to die if I were not to do it. Even with the innermost sincerity of my whole being I was not able to get at it, and the situation was unbearable. Yet with love and determination, eagerness and courage, I started on my journey. I had to get through different stages and places in the undertaking.

Being quite deft, it would not allow me cognition, at first. But lo, I saw it today, I was sure, but the very next moment I felt perhaps it was not it. Whenever I saw it I was intent on observing it keenly, but not knowing its nature with certitude, could not decide either way. I could not be sure that it was my Beloved, the center of my being. Being an adept in the art of make-up, it dodged me with a quick change of form ere I could arrive at a conclusion. These were the visions of various Incarnations of Rishis and Saints, internal visions in the process of Dhyana and Dharana, and external ones of the waking state eventual to the siddhis, such as the power of prophecy, clairvoyance, clairaudience, and the power to cure normally incurable diseases, etc. Some were eager to serve me, to have faith in me and to honor me, and this led me to believe that I had seen it for certain; it is here its skill in make-up lies. It is so deft in the art of changing the form, quality and knowledge, that the intellect does not know where it stands, let alone the penetration through its nature. But, what is this miracle? Wonder of wonders! The flash, curiously glistening, majestic splendor! But where is it? It disappeared in a flicker before I could apprehend it. No, nothing could be known about what happened to me or to the lightning. I could not say whether the extremely swift flash and the means of my reconnaisance were one and the same or different. In the glow of the flashing miracle the whole of the cosmic array is experienced directly. The contact is immensely interesting. The flash experience makes one feel it should be as spicy forever; this is the characteristic feeling of the cosmic experience. But in the very attempt to arrest the glowing flash for a basic understanding, one loses it. It is extremely difficult to get at the root of the cosmic energy, that perfect adept in assuming an infinite variety of forms. The consciousness to be apprehended and the power of concentration are one and the same. Being polymorphous by nature, it cannot be pinned down to any definite form or name or place, as for instance, the internal experiences of the Dhyana yogin. In the first instance, the attention of the meditator is silence in excelsis, this is transformed into light, the light assumes the form of space, the space in turn changes into movement. This is transmitted into air, and the air into fire, the fire changes into water, and the water into earth. Lastly, the earth evolves into the world of organic and inorganic things. The water from the rain takes the form of the juices in the grains and vegetables, which essences supply nourishment and energy. This energy takes the form of knowledge, courage, valor, cunning, etc. The limbless process goes on. Neither form, name, nor quality is enduring. Nothing is permanent or determinate.

The felt experience of the spiritually enlightened is difficult to negotiate with. This may mean either that it is beyond our capacity to get at, or it is beyond reach; yet one must go on with concentration. The identity of the "I" as the miracle in the process of the dazzling glitter, and the "ego" of the empirical consciousness prior to the experience, must be firmly established in Dhyana Yoga (meditation). Is the spiritually saturated soul the same as the experience or is it even beyond that? There is no duality to the experience one has in the process of Dhyana Yoga. At the enlightened stage even the sense organs are involved in the meditation of the spiritual adept, for the sense organs and the five elements are one and the same at the core. The material elements, subtle matter and consciousness, the three qualities, Satva, Rajas and Tamas, and the three sources of knowledge, perception, inference and testimony were seen, are being seen, and lo! They are not there.

The characteristics of origination, sustenance and destruction come under Dhyana Yoga itself. The activity of Prakriti in all its forms, manifest and unmanifest, and the consciousness of Purusha are also included in it. In the Dhyana Yoga process the eight chakras are activated simultaneously and are experienced as such. All these, in a single, unitive experience, I constitute the contemplation. Meditation, consciousness, experience, are all but a single unity.

Dhyana Yoga is the supreme activity of life. Concentration is the central thing in experience.

The transformation of Dhyana Yoga into Mama [sic] Yoga is a difficult process. In the consummation of this process alone is the Atman cognized with certitude. As long as Dhyana Yoga is not completely transformed into Jnana Yoga, so long there is no Self knowledge. The test of Dhyana is knowledge, then follows the duality of knowledge and the Atman. In the experiential knowledge, there is a race between knowledge as Self and Self as Self. But in deep samadhi there is an understanding between contemplation and the Self. This results in the realization of bliss. The bliss is transformed into supreme beatitude and the self is absorbed in the supreme Spirit. Knowledge to itself, contemplation into itself, the primal Maya, God, the Absolute state and the original throb are all a single whole of Self-experience. The ever cherished and desired Being is realized here. # Self Knowledge and Self Realization

Prior to this, in the process of the attainment of the siddhis incidental to Dhyana Yoga, there ooze forth experiences in the form of arts, love, and memories of past lives in different regions such as Patala, Swarga and Kailas. In some cases one has a taste of different siddhis and Avatars and of a series of meetings with others in different regions. There are experiences of being the Brahma of Satya region, Shiva of Kailas, and Vishnu of Vaikunth from time immemorial. Again, there are different phases of the yogin's feelings, the best and the worst, and the endless panoramas, not pleasant nor enduring; and the inevitable adjuncts of Dhyana Yoga must go on until it is transformed into Jnana Yoga; i.e., the transition from the Samprajuata (silent mind in meditation) to the Asamprajuata (altered state of consciousness, silent and alert mind) state of samadhi. Until then there is no Self-realization. But, on the other hand, if in the process of this transition the nature of this phase of Dhyana Yoga be known, Self-realization is automatic.

All the experiences and visions arising out of Dhyana Yoga are transitory. In the contemplation, there is an infinite variety of phases and forms, and none of them is lasting. Whatever is taken to be helpful and great and determinate vanishes in an instant and a new form takes its place to yield place to the next. That knowledge from which all the varieties issue forth in experiences, such as earth, water, fire, air, ether, and their various specifications, is itself unstable. Starting from meditation, the contemplating soul, having experienced a taste of previous lives, is further transformed into the primal Maya, primordial energy, and Godhead, and even into the characteristics of the supreme Self by the power of meditation, and all this for a trice, and it disappears. It is here that it is called Kala, the final liquidation of individuality. It is here that the separation from itself is compensated for, and finds itself with spiritual certitude, never to be lost again. The imperishable, indissoluble, eternal Paramatman shines forth with perfection beyond the reach of empirical experience.

KNOW WHAT?

The continuous process of getting to know the environment goes on from the birth of the "I" consciousness. Though the "I" consciousness is automatic, hence effortless, one has to learn to do various things; one also must learn about one's own person and its care. Some things are mastered of necessity, and of one's liking; others which are not essential must also be learnt.

In the process of conscious learning, over and above the world of things, we are told we must also learn of the things beyond the world; but before trying to know the things beyond, we must know the controller and support of the universe called God, so that other things may be known with His help.

Who is God and how is He to be propitiated? We are told that this is to be achieved by forming friendship with saintly persons and by regularly and devoutly carrying out their instructions; but then, we are told, it is a matter of rare good fortune that one comes across such a saintly soul, and when one comes across such a person, by rare good fortune, the saintly soul tells us, "You yourself are God. Think of Him alone, meditate on His being. Do not engage yourself in thinking of anybody else."

For a while I used to deal with various matters and perform activities such as knowing and learning with the idea that I was a human being, born of the "I" consciousness; next I started meditating on myself as God in order to know myself. Now I know that I am the knower of whatever I remember, perceive, or feel; hence, ignoring all that is remembered, perceived, or felt, I contemplate on the nature of the knower.

I am sitting in a secluded place where none can see me, with my eyes half closed. Whatever I remember, perceive, feel or experience comes into being from within myself. My meditation is my torch and what I see is its light, all that I see and remember is just the light of my meditation.

Now I do not feel the necessity to meditate anymore, for the nature of meditation is such that it is spontaneous. In its process, it gives rise to innumerable forms and names and qualities....and what have I got to do with it all?

Now I am convinced beyond doubt that this meditation of mine is born of God; and the world of things is the product of my meditation only. The cyclic process of origination, sustenance and destruction is the very core of the world's being. However more I may try to know, the same process must repeat. My inquisitiveness has come to an end.

SPIRITUAL BLISS

The spiritual aspirant is absorbed in his spiritual experiments and experiences, and the journey continues. One already has the experience of the world through his senses, hence he tries, as far as possible, to depend only on himself, he tries to gauge the extent to which he can go with the minimum of help from others and eschews the use of many things in the world. In due course, the aspirant is sure to win peace; nothing is wanting, he has enough and to spare. He is satisfied and his behavior reveals it. He expects nothing from those with whom he deals. Is expecting material returns from others any different from begging? If it is true that he has attained to happiness beyond the reach of ordinary mortals, why should he expect a beggarly share from material gains? If he has in his possession the blissful spring of eternal life, why should he ask a price from his dealings with others? It is impossible that one who has realized his Self should rely on others; on the contrary, he feeds others on spiritual food with absolute ease.

As the happiness of the people increases, they begin to love him with greater sincerity, they know his importance in their lives. Just as they acquire and store food, so too they take care of one who has attained the position of eternal peace, identity with the universal spirit, perfection. Yet some people get to know some occult processes from great Saints and practice them, enabling them to acquire certain occult powers and they are misled into thinking they have what they have been striving for, and style themselves as Raja yogins, and engage in the avid pursuit of material pleasures; but one who has tasted the pure bliss of eternal life in Brahman is forever satisfied, the perfect soul does not desire worldly honors.

It is impossible that the spiritually perfect soul should ever desire to be called the preceptor or to make others bow down before him or to expect all to honor his word in every respect. One who gets the highest kind of happiness from his life source has no interest in material happiness. That is spiritual happiness which makes everyone happy. These are the external qualities characterizing the enlightened satyagrahin (seeker of truth).

THE TENDER HEART OF THE SAINT

The heart of a mother is full of tenderness, but it is limited to her child only; but the heart of the Saint is all inclusive, it knows the how and whence of the origin of each one and the vicissitudes they have to go through.

The Saint is full of spiritual knowledge and pacific repose, there is nothing wanting. He practices his sadhana in such a way as not to be discovered by others; he has no use for the external marks of saintliness, he dresses in keeping with the time and climate.

Being in touch with the atom, the first cause of the universe, he knows its nature quite well. Blossoming forth is the very nature of the core of this atom, hence changes and differentiation are bound to be there. Knowing this well, the Saint is neither elated by pleasing events nor depressed by the opposite ones.

He has gauged the depth of the knowledge of the common man. He knows its nature from beginning to end. He knows the how and the why of the mentality, also the worthlessness of its achievements and failures. The needs of the body prompt the creature to acquire means of sustenance, but the greed for these makes the creature pursue them to the point of uselessness, and all of this without the least idea of what awaits the life in future. What the creature deems essential and strives to acquire, the Saint knows to be sheer trash.

The Saint is never a victim of passions. Life is a mixture of passions and emotions; Atman, the origin of passions and emotions, is the very core of the Saint's vision, the nature of which he is thoroughly acquainted. He knows its activities and varieties of manifestation, as well as their consequences. The life principle is the principle of feelings, passions, emotions. Desires and passions engendered in this principle are just emotive experiences, they have nothing of substance in them; yet the poor creature thinks them to be of great significance in his life, embraces the basically worthless desires, indulges in sense enjoyment, and runs after them helplessly.

The mother, with sincerity but in ignorance, feeds the roots of misery, while the Saint, with the same intensity, weeds them out. The Saint knows what the welfare of the people lies in much better than does the mother of her child. That is why the heart of the Saint is said to be kind.

DEVOTION TO BALAKRISHNA AND HIS CARE

During the process of Bhakta, Bhajan, and renunciation, the experience of the immensity of God is on the increase, but as the vision becomes more frequent, it gets narrower day by day. Here vision and knowledge are identical. In whatever name and form God is propitiated, that name and form he presents himself in. The various forms and names are woven into prayers and hymns and are sung by the common man.

The devotee by his firm determination, and God by his fascination for devotion, are attracted to each other and the moment they come face to face they merge; the devotee loses his phenomenal consciousness automatically, and when it returns he finds that he has lost his identity, lost into that of God and can never be separated again; God everywhere and no separate identity.

The creator, enjoyer, and destroyer of all names and forms, the controller of all powers, is revealed now; this is God, the Self, Self-luminous, Self-inspired, and Self-conscient. Here is where the primal gunas originate. Though atomic in character, he has in him the absolute power to do what he wills, in accordance with the emotive character of the gunas, and to take any form. This is the atomic center, atomic energy, the first and final cause of the universe.

The God of Gods, the soul of the movable and immovable, the all-pervasive, qualified Brahman, the beloved of the Bhaktas, the ocean of love and devotion is born here. This is Adinarayana, residing in the hearts of the devotees; the Saints call him Balakrishna (Baby Krishna), for in the beginning he is seen to be the atom of atoms. By nature, he is innocence incarnate. He is easily moved by emotions and becomes many (immense), in accordance with the direction taken by the emotions. The nature of the expansion is determined by the excess of one or another of the three gunas. He manifests himself through each of the three gunas at different times in a non-partisan spirit. As the Saints are closely acquainted with him, they know what guna he would induce at any given moment and what the consequences would be, and hence they dissuade him from the excess of his nature. Excess of growth in any guna is dangerous. Satva guna is absolutely good, yet even that is harmful when hypertrophied; Rajas is restless and overbearing, while Tamas is blind and arrogant. Knowing this well, the wise man keeps his soul away from the effects of the gunas, hence the energy of the soul remains undiminished and develops in the right direction.

Satisfying various desires increases the taste for them, and the thirst for enjoyment slowly decreases the power of the soul in imperceptible degrees, but when, setting aside the temptation of the gunas, the devotee finds his pure soul, he fondly takes to its rearing with love and sincerity; only when the devotion is successful is the Atman realized. He is seen as a child at the dawn of victory, hence he is called the child of victory.

The Bhakta is alert not to allow it to be polluted by the craving for sensuous pleasures; the firmer it is in its nature, the greater becomes the power and strength of the soul, hence the Saints do not allow it to lose its steadiness. The crux of rearing it lies in keeping it firm, undeflected by the presence of the gunas. If the spiritual gain of the soul be eclipsed by sensuous desires, it is shaken to its very roots. It is difficult to keep the gunas at rest, that is why the Saints advise stabilizing in Self-knowledge.

Those who have realized and stabilized in Self-knowledge are those whose glory is sung from time immemorial; it is their names that form the basis of divine meditation. Sri Krishna, Sri Vishnu, and Sri Rama are some of the innumerable names given to God; originally, these were the names given to the human form, but they became Self-realized and came to know the root cause of all experience. Those who came to possess this knowledge of the Self and kept it pure and secure are known to be Gods and Saints, while those who utilized it for the sake of sense enjoyment are called devils and Ravanas.

The highest and rarest gain is difficult of achievement, but, if achieved, it is superlatively beneficent, and if not properly cared for, is equally harmful. One who does not get excited by the possession of spiritual knowledge of the root cause can, with love and devotion, cultivate and brighten it. Devotion and prayer and renunciation are firmly established in him, he is always free from desires, and wherever he is the aura of peace and happiness is about him; the auriole shown about the heads of great Saints is a pictorial representation of this fact. Whoever approaches him gets an unsolicited touch of the divine bliss. The Saint never acts as an individual, all his actions are the expression of the divine Lila.

SPIRITUAL KNOWLEDGE AND THE PACIFICATION OF THE DESIRE TO KNOW

This universe came into being through the activity of the primal atomic (atmic) consciousness. There was nothing, not even a trace of appearance before self-consciousness, and in this state there came into being the consciousness of one's own existence, the awareness of one's own being. In fact, there was no time, nor space, nor cause. The awareness has no cause for it, hence it is futile to name one. There was no time, hence it cannot be dated. There was no space, hence its location is meaningless; yet the atomic consciousness was felt as such and nothing more why so? For there was nothing over and above it to be aware of! The awareness only of being was there. How long this state lasted, there are no means to ascertain; but the great miracle is that the self-consciousness was there; with it was the cosmic will, followed by its realization. The atomic consciousness, on account of its will and its instant realization, became many and pervasive. Although apparently many, it is all one in essence.

When the atomic consciousness became many and pervasive on account of its will and its instantaneous realization, the energy of the single atom diversified itself into many centers, each with its own peculiarity and will; hence the conflict. At any given moment, the innumerable centers express their will in a variety of ways; generally, the willing atom does not know the "whither" and "what" of its will, but the effect is bound to be there. The tangible result of the wills of the willing atoms is to be witnessed at the moment of cosmic destruction, when the whole universe is reduced to ashes. The loving wills are not cancelled altogether; the great moments of happiness in the world are the result of these wills. The characteristic of the individual energy to will is always operative. It is its essence and it owes it to the primordial energy.

The primal energy that scintillated first is one and homogenous, but appears to be heterogenous due to ignorance.

The quivering atomic energy is designated as the Great Principle by the Vedantas: the essential characteristic of the Principle is consciousness. The felt awareness expands itself into ether, the expanse of the ether is the space. With a single quality this Great Principle became time, space and cause. Next came the three gunas and the five elements. The speed was simply immeasurable.

The original scintillation moved in space and that was the air, the air gathered momentum and fire came into existence. The throbbing of the fire increased and became cold and that was water; the water cooled even more and that was earth. All the characteristics of the previous forms are crystallized in the earth and vibrate there; in virtue of this peculiarity there came into being innumerable varieties of living beings and vegetation, and the original quiver pulsates in and through their vital sap. The original will pervades the whole range of moving and immovable things and is constantly active there.

The scintillating characteristic prior to ether is filling every electron and proton and is constantly increasing in strength. As long as the quiver in the atoms is operative, so long the constituents must be in motion. The original will pervades the whole range of moving and immovable beings and is constantly active there.

The original consciousness sees nothing except itself. It has no organs, yet it is in action with innumerable Spiritual Knowledge and the Pacification of the Desire to Know 131 organs. It is never polluted. The various conscious centers hedged by the limiting adjuncts only think they are different from the original source, but there is only one being, one spirit, one quality; formless, timeless, non-spatial, the one, pure consciousness. There is no scope for difference or distinction. The creature, deluded by the narrow interests of "I" and "mine", suffers pain for nothing, it is limited only to itself. Everything takes place at the proper moment, in accordance with the law that binds all, and everything materializes at the proper moment. When Ravana becomes unbearable Rama is there to give relief. When Kamsa rules supreme, Krishna is there as an antidote. This is how the rhythm of ups and downs is maintained.

The controlling force of all these events is the same, it never changes. It cannot be that there is one God in one age and another in another age.

Just a single quality gives birth to the glow of the expanded universe; in the absence of that one quality, all is pure silence. When this one single quality is known and befriended, the heart mingles with the Heart; there is that supreme sense of inalienable mutuality of oneness of quality in all, and all as belonging to the One. The supreme unity is realized; hence it is called the Supreme Self.

All time, all space and all cause have become one for eternity, the One alone is all-active. It has no gain nor loss nor death. It is unborn, eternal, and yet is born every moment and manifests itself in every epoch. All spiritual and intellectual knowledge comes to rest here.

THE GAYATRI HYMN

"The Hymn of hymns, oh Uddhava, is the Gayatri hymn. I shall explain it to thee from the beginning to end; pray hear." (Ekanathi Bhagawata XXI).

The Lord says, "Oh Uddhava, Gayatri hymn is the bedrock of all hymns." All means many. That in virtue of which this number comes to be experienced is Gayatri. The tri-syllabic A+U+M means Omkar - The Logos. The next step starts with two numbers. The first one is the consciousness of one's own being. It is the natural characteristic, the unuttered word. It is the unknowingly spoken word given out everywhere and every moment and no one knows about it. This word, uttered unawares, is the Gayatri hymn, the basis of all hymns. Innumerable words are spoken subsequently; and all the universes spring from them, but the prime source of all is the Gayatri Chhandas, the unspoken word, the unuttered sound. Everyone has the same experience, and what is the experience born of this unspoken word? One's own being.

There are innumerable varieties of being from the ant to the gods, but what is the original being? It is Gayatri. The experience of this being is one's own being. This Gayatri Chhandas comes first, the rest only follows. The characteristic of that being is explained by the Lord as follows: "What is the nature of that hymn? Even though there be the power to create innumerable universes, it cannot be left hold of." The original sound of the unasked for, unspoken, unthought of and unuttered word was born in the form of Chakrapani and it is unique to him; but not recognizing it, the Perfect has come to be a deplorable creature through graded degeneration in the course of the temporal process.

The pursuit of the Chhandas is fascinating. For everyone, it is the same awareness of being, the unspoken word, yet spoken. In spite of the efforts of the four Vedas, six Shastras and eighteen Puranas, its interpretation remains incomplete ? Still there is the uninterrupted fascination for the Gayatri Chhandas.

What does Gayatri Chhandas mean? It is the awareness of your own being, it is whatever you understand without speech. Wherever there is life, there is the hymn to support it. It vibrates in us, and in spite of years of miserable drudgery, we do not feel like parting with it. In virtue of this Gayatri hymn Sri Rama and Sri Vishnu came to this earth as incarnations, but they mastered it. This unwitting consciousness of your own being is the same in us and in them, but they did it consciously and experienced it as such. Other beings get only to the surface of the meaning, which is only a perversion thereof; the yawning of the creatures lets out the syllables A+U+M.

Meditate on the meaning as you have understood above. You are Chakrapani, the being with a thousand hands and heads, the unuttered sound. The word and its resounding sense are the first Person, and are experienced as such.

The sign of the experience is complete satisfaction of the mind. Gayatri hymn is the substratum of the satisfaction of all and it bursts forth spontaneously, for the sound is ever glorious. The name that resounds in you without being uttered is your own indwelling spirit.

It is enough if you silently listen to the ten sounds, five resoundings, dual reverberation and the single voice, and the symphony of them all. This basic Gayatri hymn is with you only.

Three groups of eight syllables make one series of twenty-four sounds. Gayatri Mantra consists of twenty-four syllables as follows: Oam, Bhooh, Oam, Bhuvah, Oam, Swaha, Oam, Mahah, Oam, Janah, Oam, Tapah, Oam, Satyam, Tat, Savituih, Varenyam, Bhargah, Devasya, Dhimahi, Dhiyo, Yo, Nah, Prachodayaat. Great Rishis and Saints acquire immense power by reciting this hymn of twenty-four syllables. Innumerable worlds are created and destroyed by its power, but consider the power of the bisyllabic word Rama that easily cancels all this power and rests in perfection.

VEDAS AS BASIC: They were basic to the subsequent interpretation, hence they are called basic, but the primal root, first cause of everything is this hymn.

THE BEATITUDE OF BRAHMAN: The experience of one's own being, of the vision of one's own Self and the eventual peace that is unparallelled is called Brahmananda. The experience of one's own nature without the help of others is later on interpreted as the Great Beatitude, (Paramananda).

SPIRITUAL LIFE: Just as there is the luster of luster, so also is Gayatri Chhandas the very life of spirit. The Lord says, "I am hidden and it is my treasure, but that which hides me also reveals me. How do I appear when seen? Surely as non-dual, non-different. He who listens to the vibrating hymn is hidden. With the devout recitation of this hymn everything will be distinctly clear, for it is already there; but if one wishes to realize my vision without it, he will have it, and it will be Advaita - non-dual." (The reference is to Nama yoga as an easy alternative to Dhyana or Raja Yoga.) What do the syllables of this immovable one signify? Absolute bliss of the Self, it is Sat (being), Chit (consciousness), and Ananda (beatitude). This is the essence of the Gayatri hymn. Its contemplation confers absolute bliss.

FLORAL OFFERINGS FROM NISARGADATTA

Feeding, rest and sex-life give rise to the experience of life, world and the Brahman. The path of devotion is eternal imperishable. Devotion should be practised devoutly. Spiritual knowledge should be attained with conscious efforts. That consciousness which makes us aware of knowledge should be utilised for spiritual knowledge. The world is born of our will. The awareness that is at the root of this experience is nothing but our own self. The characteristics and form of the awareness must be known.

Whatever appears is evanescent for it is not there at all. Palatial buildings and Palaces that we see today were not there before. The "perceivable" presupposes the percipient. But the percipient soul is different from the perceived. It is imperishable and formless. The "I" that is different from the "eyed" must be known directly. The individual takes the supreme soul to be an individual.

The knowledge that makes this experience possible is nothing different from the experiencing "I". But that which is prior, even to this experience is known as the supreme Soul. The awareness that makes experience possible is called knowledge.

Knowledge is God and the witness thereof is the supreme Soul.

"What do you know of God beyond the word itself"?

If you think that you are a Jnanin now, you are utterly mistaken then; may be, you are that, but so long as you have not given up all desires, you are not a real Jnanin. All that you know is only verbal knowledge.

If you mean to talk about spiritual knowledge on the strength of the intellect, be sure, you will never gain

happiness and peace for the intellect is absolutely helpless before the Pure Spirit.

"I am luminous, I am like ether, I am formless, pure and bodiless". This should be your intense and speechless meditation every day, before going to sleep at least. And in course of time you will certainly attain to the state. This is what your Guru says; do not forget it. Whatever you intently meditate on in the hypnoidal state you are sure to realise.

How possibly could the world go on if the spiritually enlightened were to isolate themselves from it?

There is nothing excepting the word "God"; but that should not hinder you in your firm resolve. Even if you have realised yourself, do not give up meditation or prayer or worship for knowledge devoid of devotion is colourless. Whatever the enlightened speak, they do so in a state of spiritual intoxication. Hence, they do not care for anything, even for themselves. Whatever such a soul says in the state of divine inspiration he is absolutely unaware of. Hence, he is not proud of it. He knows that whether it be Rama or Krishna or anybody else and whatever his status as a philosopher, he is after all a product of name and form.

If God were to meet only at the time of death, then all efforts are in vain.

The Guru is with you now, serve him with care. Meditate on what you have heard and on your knowledge too. If you do not remember it then keep quiet. God intuits about himself as God what you intuit about yourself. He is aware of his godliness only as a correlate of the devotee. If the awareness in virtue of which you have this cognition (i. e. of God) is not there, who can say “this is God” then? Your awareness of yourself is the God’s awareness of his godliness. Hence, be sure that what you need, God also needs.

Keep your mind under your control, fix it firmly at the feet of the Guru and be the master of your own mind.

The awareness of your being is the treasure of the formless supreme Spirit. Whatever status you raise it to, will be yours; but not of your physical frame. When you meditate on the form of Guru, it enters into your being; In the process of this meditation the determinate form emerges from your formless being. This is what is known as the form of God. If the reference be masculine, it is Bhagwana and if feminine, it is Bhagawati. The form of your vision, be it that of Datta or of Vishnu or of any other divinity, it springs forth only from your own formless being.

It is all sheer superstition to think that messengers of Vishnu are commissioned for escorting the meritorious and those of Yama, for the sinful at the time of death. If none has accompanied us at the time of birth it is an idle gossip to say that there would be one at the time of departure.

You soul will manifest itself in whatever status you raise it is. Meditate on and worship your soul as the Sadguru and you are sure to attain to that status; but you are not to be identified with your body.

No devotee has ever had the experience of God or Guru as different from self-knowledge.

It is a matter of faith. "Faith is always fruitful". Faith is a great thing. The faith in our own being is itself the feet of guru; once you are firm in this faith of yours, visiting other gods and goddesses is superfluous.

9 789348 143044

Printed at Repro India Ltd.